Families Around the World

Australia ▪ France ▪ China

by
Don Massey

Reidmore Books Inc.

Don Massey is a professor in the Department of Elementary Education at the University of Alberta. He is the author of several elementary social studies textbooks, including Reidmore's Canada, Its Land and People.

Pedagogical Consultants

Reidmore Books would like to thank Doris Severyn and Theresa Pond for their advice and assistance during the development of *Families Around the World*. Also, thanks goes to the following teachers who field tested *Families Around the World* in their classrooms: Elaine Iacononi, Glenise Harvey, and Joyce Lukasewich of Baturyn School, Edmonton. The following teachers, from Holy Family School, Edmonton, offered insights and assistance: Rose Papianni, Cathy Sitke, Nancy Dixon, and Edith McEwan.

Content Validators

China:
Dr. Brian Evans,
Vice-President, Academic
The University of Alberta
Edmonton, Alberta

Australia:
Mr. Robert Pounds
Information Officer
Office of the Australian High Commission
Ottawa, Ontario

France
Diane Legros and Marie-Helen de la Chenelière
Project Coordinators
Les Éditions de la Chenelière
Montreal, Quebec

Credits

Typesetting & Design: Pièce de Résistance Ltée., Edmonton, AB
Illustrations and Maps: Pièce de Résistance Ltée., Edmonton, AB

Reidmore Books gratefully acknowledges the assistance and the cooperation of the following individuals, agencies, and corporations in providing the visuals and information used in this book:

Abbreviations

CIDA Canadian International Development Agency

Entries are by page number, coded as follows: T = Top B = Bottom L = Left R = Right

7R, 9T&B, Dr. Jim Wicks (Courtesy, Goodman Family)
8, 10, 11T&B, 13, 14,15, 16T&B, 17, 19, 20L&R Courtesy, Australian High Commission
12 Tom Price (Courtesy, Australian High Commission)
15BL Australian Tourist Commission (Courtesy, Australian High Commission)
25, 26, 27, 28, 29, 30, 32, 33, 34 Michel de la Chenelière
36, 40, 42, 43, 45 Wu Zhou
37, 38T&B, 39, 41, 44 George Palacky
46 CIDA

We have made every effort to correctly identify and credit the sources of all photographs, illustrations, and information used in this textbook. Reidmore Books appreciates any further information or corrections; acknowledgment will be given in subsequent editions.

The publisher gratefully acknowledges financial support from the Alberta Foundation for the Literary Arts.

REIDMORE
BOOKS
INC

Canadian Cataloguing in Publication Data

Massey, Donald L., 1936-
Families around the world

ISBN 0-919091-48-2

1. Family - Juvenile literature. I. Title. HQ734.M37 1988 j306.8'5 C88-091433-5

printed and bound in Canada

Contents

Getting Ready to Read

What do these signs say to you?

As you read this book, you will see more signs. The signs tell you what you will read about.

Look at the signs and meanings listed below. People all around the world have their own ways of doing the things shown in the signs. As you read *Families Around the World*, you will learn about how people meet their needs, and in this way, you will learn more about how you meet your own needs.

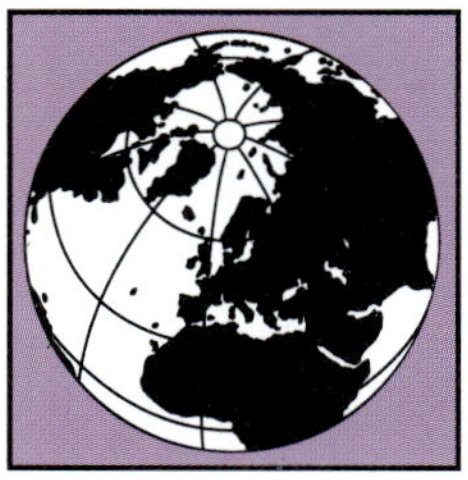

This sign tells you about where people live.

This sign tells you about how children learn in other countries and what kinds of schools they go to.

This sign tells you about how people and **loads** are moved. Moving from place to place happens in many ways.

This sign tells you about animals.

This sign tells you about homes.

This sign tells you about foods that are eaten.

This sign tells you about sports that are played and about other ways that people have fun.

This sign tells you about clothes that are worn.

The Goodman Family

Kelly and Sara Goodman live in **Perth**. Perth is a city in a country called **Australia**.

Australia is in the southern half of the world. It is a country and a **continent**.

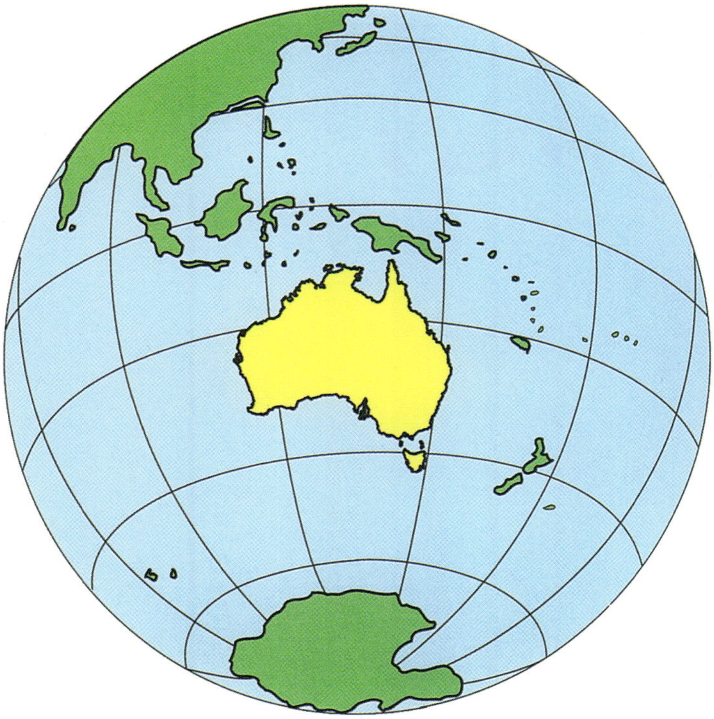

This map shows where Australia is in the world.

Kelly and Sara can see the Indian Ocean from their backyard. A cool breeze blows in from the ocean. On hot days, this makes it comfortable.

Most people in Australia live near the ocean. With such a big country, places are often far apart.

Why do you think people live along the coast?

What Is School Like?

Kelly and Sara with their classmates. Why do you think the girls wear uniforms?

Kelly and Sara go to school in Perth. Everyone at their school wears a **uniform**.

"Our school uniforms have the name of our school printed on them," said Sara.

There are many schools in Perth. Kelly and Sara's school is close to home, so the girls can ride their bikes there.

How do you go to school?

Kelly and Sara's friends, Jamie, Brian, and Amanda Murray live on a ranch. They call it a **station**.

Stations are surrounded by countryside. There are no nearby schools. Every day the Murrays go to "School of the Air." A teacher gives out lessons and homework "over the air" on the radio. The children sit near the radio and listen to their school lessons.

Jamie, Brian, and Amanda are doing their school lessons. Do you think that Sara and Kelly learn the same things as Jamie, Brian, and Amanda? Why?

In both schools, students learn about Australia. Some of the things they learn about are shown on this page.

This is a picture of the Australian coat of arms. Ask your teacher to show you a picture of your country's coat of arms.

These are pictures of Australian coins and notes.

These are pictures of stamps used in Australia.

How are these things different from what you learn about? How are they the same as the things you learn about?

How Are People And Loads Moved?

"Dad, may we visit the Murrays at their station?" asked Kelly.

"Okay," said Dad. "The next time I drive out that way, you may come along."

Dad is a truck driver. He transports sheep for farmers.

People travel in many ways in Australia. How do people travel where you live?

Mr. Goodman's truck. What are big trucks used for?

Markets for sheep, beef cattle, wheat, and sugar may be far away. Special trucks, trains, and ships have been built for moving these bulky loads.

Early the next morning the Goodmans began their trip to visit the Murrays.

"Look at that sign, girls," said Mom. "We are driving through an area where animals live."

What do you think this sign means? What animal road signs have you seen?

What Animals Are Seen?

The Goodmans see **koalas** asleep in the trees.

They see hikers with a **wombat**.

Kangaroos hop across the grass.

Where have you seen these animals?

What Are Homes Like?

This is the Goodman home.

This is the Murray home. How are these two homes the same? How are they different?

These homes were built to be cool. They have **verandahs**. On hot days, the verandah is a cool place to sit.

On the Murray's sheep station, workers care for the sheep.

What care do animals need?

The sheep are **sheared** for their wool. Wool is **woven** and made into clothes.

What Foods Are Eaten?

The Murrays and the Goodmans enjoy a **barbecue** on the station.

Mr. Murray likes to cook this way. He puts steaks on the grill. Sometimes he puts potatoes in tin foil. There are berries and bananas for dessert.

What kind of weather is best for a barbecue? In what ways is their barbecue similar to ones you have seen? How is it different?

What Sports Are Played?

At dinner, the Murrays and Goodmans talk about some of the sports played in Australia.

What sport is being played in this picture? What kind of weather is best for this sport?

The seasons are different in Australia. Kelly and Sara's summer holiday starts in mid-December. It lasts until the end of January. At Christmas, they often go to the beach.

They do not have a winter like we do. There is a cooler season in July and August. The weather in Australia lets people play many sports.

What kinds of sports are being played in these pictures? What kinds of sports do you like to play?

The Goodmans and Murrays like sports. The sunny weather, ocean, river, and parks make Australia a big playground.

Many people in Australia like outdoor sports. They fish. They play football, **rugby**, **soccer**, **tennis**, and **cricket**. Their sailboat racers are some of the fastest in the world.

The Goodmans and Murrays agreed that there were many fun sports to play in Australia.

The Louvat Family

The Louvat (lü va) family lives in a town. The name of their town is Pacy-sur-Eure (pa sē sur ėr), but people who live there call the town Pacy. Pacy is in a country called France.

The people in France speak a language called French. You will learn some French words as you read this story. The French word for Mother is Maman and the French word for Father is Papa.

This is the Louvat family. Jean and his brother Paul play boules (bül). Their Maman and Papa join in.

France is a country in the northern part of the world.

It is on the continent called **Eurasia**.

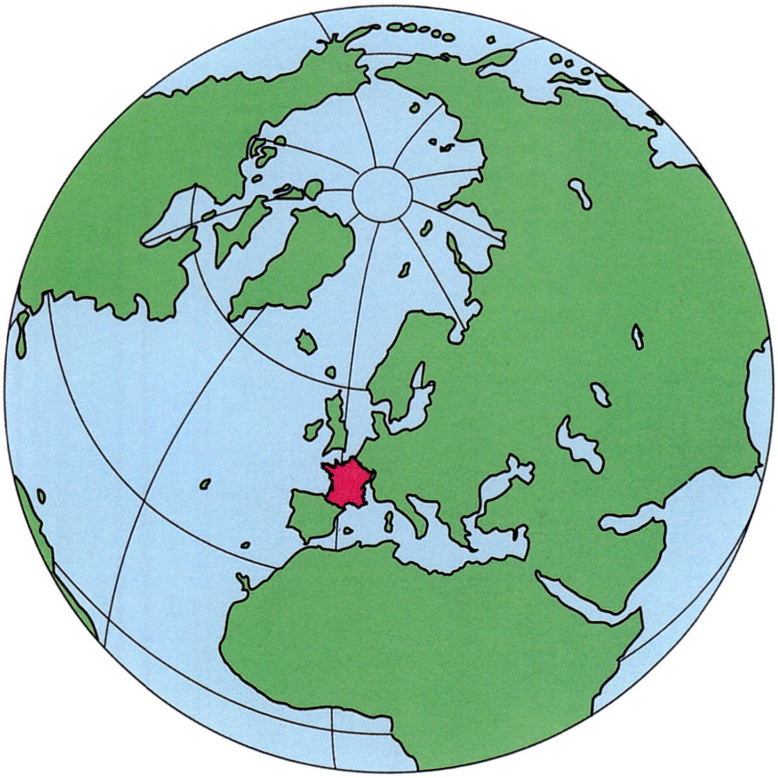

This is a map that shows where France is in the world.

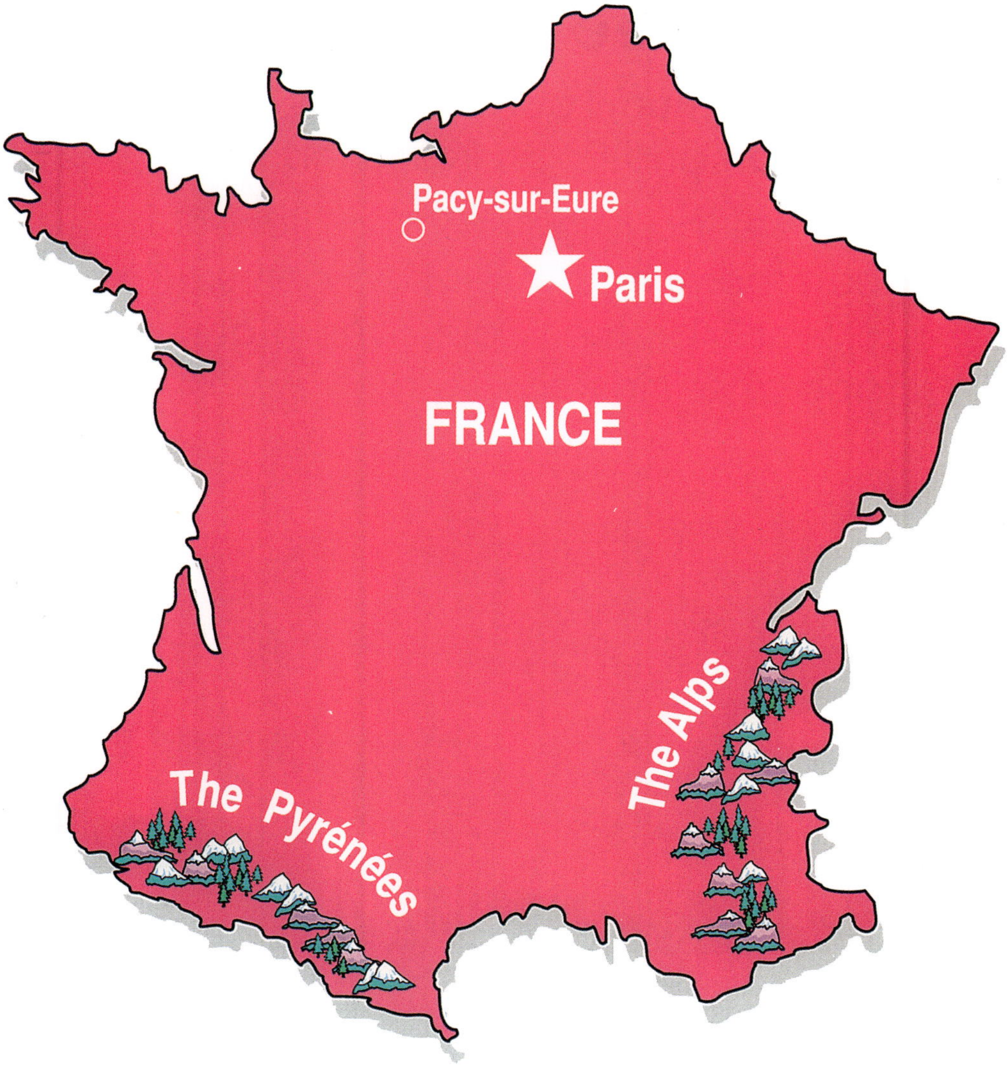

1. Run your finger along the tops of these mountains:
   - The Alps
   - The Pyrénées (Pē rā nā)
2. Find Pacy-sur-Eure.
3. Find Paris.

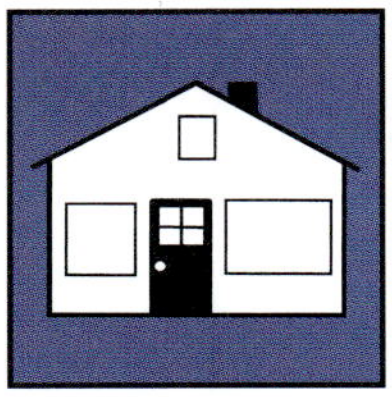

What Are Homes Like?

Jean (zhun) Louvat and his Maman and Papa live in this house.

There is a living room, a kitchen, a bathroom, and three bedrooms.

Jean's brother, Paul, lives in an apartment in Pacy.

Why do you think this house was built the way it is?

Here are some other kinds of homes where people live in France.

Which of these kinds of homes would you like to live in?

Do you know anyone who lives in an apartment?

What do you call homes that are built side by side as these are?

Some families in France live in a house. How is this house the same as your home? How is it different?

This is a château. Would you like to live in a château? Why or why not?

Few people live in a **château** (sha tō). These big houses have many rooms. They were built long ago.

A Walk With Jean

Jean is old enough to go to places in town alone. Almost every week he goes to the video store.

Along the way there are things to see. Big machines are fun to watch. Sometimes the noise makes him cover his ears. There is always work being done in town.

Jean often meets his Papa at the train station. The station is a busy place. Sometimes Jean buys chocolate at the news-stand where his Papa buys a newspaper.

One day Jean saw people painting a building. He was surprised when their work turned out to be a real painting.

Think of a title for each of the pictures on these two pages. For each picture, think of one question that you would like to ask Jean. Share your question with a classmate.

What Foods Are Eaten?

Jean shops at the market with his Maman. A market is a group of stores that each sell special foods.

First they stop at the **charcuterie** (shar ku trē). It is the pork butcher shop. They buy a small roast.

"I also want some fresh vegetables," said Maman. She and Jean walk to the **marché** (mar shā).

They look for tomatoes, peppers, lettuce, and onions for salads.

"I like to go to the market," said Jean.

"Our market is very good," said Maman.

Where does your family shop for food? How is the market in Pacy like the stores where your family shops for food? How is it different?

What food stores do you visit? What foods do you see in this picture? Are there foods here that you like to eat?

How Are People and Loads Moved?

"How does all the food get to the market?" asked Jean.

"Farmers bring the food in by truck," said Papa.

"May we visit Uncle Henri and Aunt Nanette on their farm?" asked Jean.

"Yes," said Papa. "The farm is just a short drive from town."

On the way they see fields of **grain**.

Are there grain fields near your home?

When Jean and his Papa get to the farm they see Uncle Henri at work. Uncle Henri drives a tractor into the yard. It pulls a wagon full of grain.

Sometimes grain is made into flour. What foods do you eat that are made with flour?

What can Uncle Henri and Aunt Nanette do with the things from their farm?

In the farmyard hens peck and scratch for food. Roosters march up and down. Mother hens are followed by yellow chicks. Ducks quack in the small pond. Grunts and snorts come from the pig **sty**. Cows can be seen across the field.

In the garden there are rows of carrots, beans, and peas.

"It's nice to visit the farm," said Jean. "There are so many things to see and do here. When we get home, I am going to tell my friends about the farm."

What Is Done For Fun?

When Jean and his Papa get back home, Jean goes outside to play with his friends. There are many ways to have fun in Pacy.

What are the children doing for fun in each of these pictures? Do you do the same things for fun? What other ways do you have fun?

One of Jean's favorite places is a restaurant called L'Étape (lā tap). His brother, Paul, works there.

Paul is a cook. Tonight, Paul is cooking **lobsters**.

"Let's go out for dinner tonight," said Papa.

"Hooray," said Jean.

"It will be nice to see Paul," said Maman.

This is a picture of the restaurant, L'Étape. What is your favorite restaurant?

Jean's brother is a chef. By looking at the picture can you tell what things he does at work?

At the restaurant, Jean reads the **menu** and orders a meal.

"I'll have a salad to start with. Then I'd like to have a lobster tail. I'll also have a glass of milk, please," said Jean.

Jean reads the menu. What are your favorite foods?

"**Bon appétit**," said Maman and Papa. "You have worked and played hard today. You must be very hungry!"

The Wu Family

The Wu family lives in a city called **Canton**.

Canton is in a country called the People's Republic of China.

China is in the northern part of the world. It is on the continent of Eurasia.

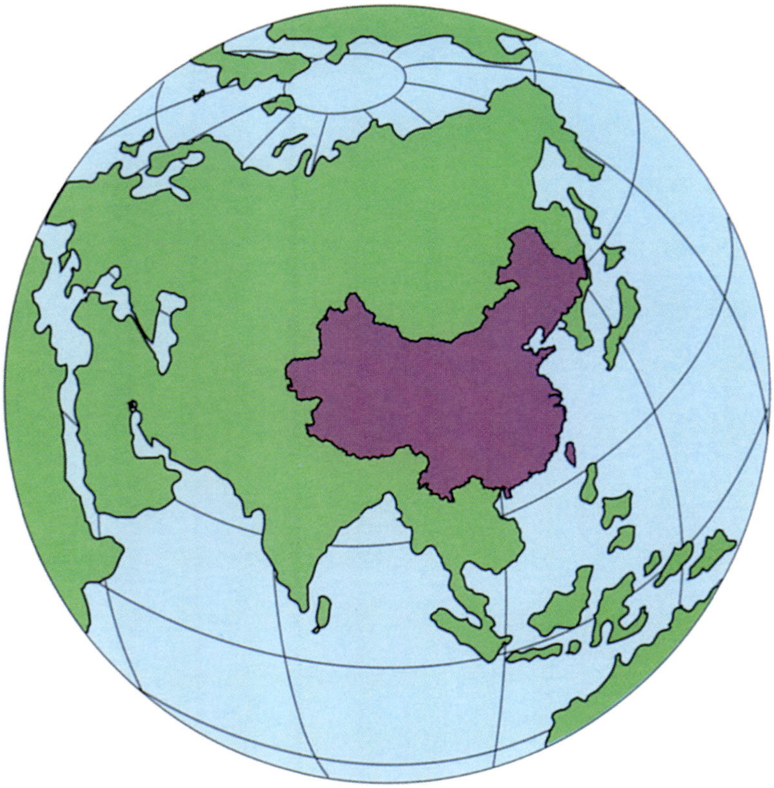

This is a map that shows where China is in the world.

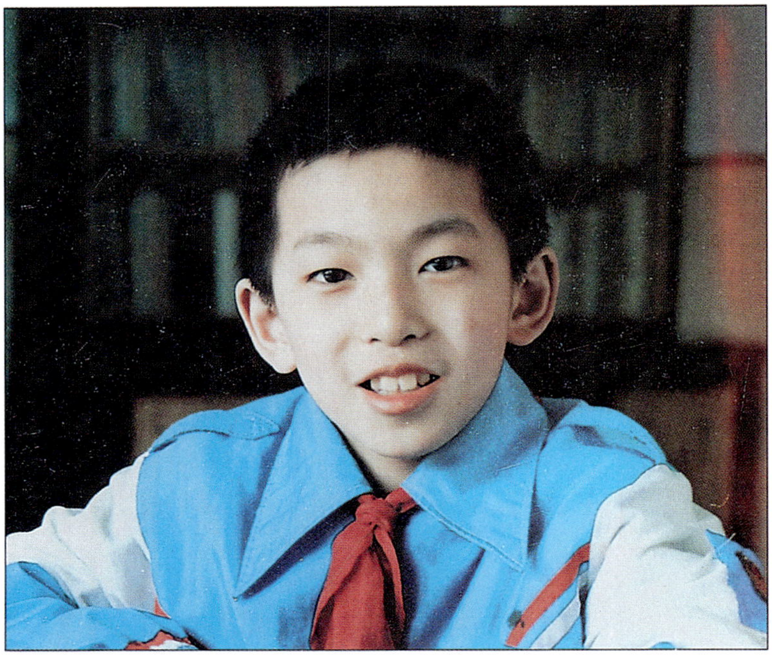

"Hello. **Ni hao**! (nē how). My name is Wu Yang. I live in a country called China. What is your country called?"

Most people call this country China.

What Are Homes Like?

How are these apartments the same as those found in your neighborhood? How are they different?

The Wu family enjoys living in their apartment. There is a main room, a small bedroom, a tiny kitchen, and a very small bathroom.

Yang lives with his mother and grandmother. Grandmother sleeps on a sofa bed in the main room.

In China, some people live in **houseboats**. Houseboats can cost less than an apartment or a house.

Why would people live in a houseboat? Would you like to live in a houseboat? Why or why not?

Some people in China live in houses. These may be single buildings or row houses.

How is this neighborhood like yours? How is it different?

What Foods Are Eaten?

Yang likes to go to the market. Outdoor markets are good places to get fresh food. They are good places to chat with neighbors. In some markets, cooked food may be bought.

People in China like to shop in the market for fresh food each day.

In what ways is this market different from where you shop?

At the apartment Grandmother steams rice. The Wu family eats many things with their rice. Tonight they will have steamed fish, sliced duck, pork, and vegetables. The food is cut into small pieces. This makes it easy to eat with **chopsticks**.

For dessert, they will have oranges.

Have you ever tried to eat with chopsticks? Can you see any other ways of eating food that are different from the way your family eats food? What ways of eating food are the same for the Wu family and your family?

The rice Yang eats is grown in the south of China. Rice is the most important food in China. Much of the land is used to grow rice. The fields are flooded so the rice can grow. Many people work in the rice fields.

What is needed to grow rice? Do you think that rice could grow in your neighborhood? Why or why not?

What Clothes Are Worn?

Most of Yang's clothing is made of **cotton** cloth. It may be made into a loose-fitting jacket and pants. In cold weather, these clothes are padded with soft cotton. Men, women, and children may be seen wearing these clothes.

When Yang goes for a walk he dresses warmly. He wears a coat to keep out the wind. He wears long pants. Yang likes to wear running shoes.

In this picture, Yang is dressed for autumn weather. What kinds of clothes do you wear in the different seasons? Do you and Yang dress the same for each season?

How Are People And Loads Carried?

What can you learn from this picture about the way people move from place to place?

When Yang walks along a city street he sees many bicycles. He sees people pulling carts and pushing wheelbarrows. He sees buses, but he sees few cars and trucks.

Yang dreams of owning a bicycle. A bicycle would help him get from place to place. What ways do you use to get from place to place?

How are loads carried where you live?
How are loads being carried in these pictures?

Yang sees loads carried in many different ways. In China, loads are carried by cart, truck, train, and airplane. Loads are also carried on small and large boats. These boats travel on the rivers and **canals**.

What Is Learned?

Yang belongs to a club called **the Young Pioneers**.

The Young Pioneers meet at school. They learn to be good citizens of China.

The Young Pioneers wear special clothes called uniforms. This tells other people who they are.

Does your club have special uniforms? How are your club uniforms the same? How are they different?

What kinds of clubs are there where you live? Do you belong to a club?

One thing that Wu Yang and the Young Pioneers learn about is animals. One of their favorite animals is the **Panda**.

The Panda lives in **bamboo** forests in China.

Do you know any special facts about Pandas? Share your facts with a friend. Do you have a favorite animal? What is it? Why is it your favorite animal?

At school Wu Yang and his classmates learn to read and write. Their language is called **Mandarin**.

Mandarin Chinese is the official language of China. In China there are many different ways to speak Chinese words, but in school all children learn to speak Mandarin.

Some Chinese words are printed below.

	Picture	Chinese Word
Mountain		山
Horse		馬
Moon		月
Field	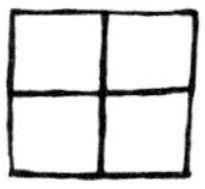	田
Rain		雨
Tree		木
River		川

How Do People Live?

In this book you read about four families. The families come from three different countries. In many ways, your own family might be the same as the Goodmans, the Murrays, the Louvats, and the Wus.

Think about how families do things.

You have learned that children around the world learn about many of the same kinds of things that you do. In some schools, children wear uniforms. You have also learned that schools are different in other countries. What would you like to learn more about after reading this book?

You have learned about how people and loads are moved. People around the world move loads by truck, cart, train, car, and airplane. Can you think of other ways of moving people and loads?

You have learned that there are different kinds of animals in different countries. What are some animals that live in your country?

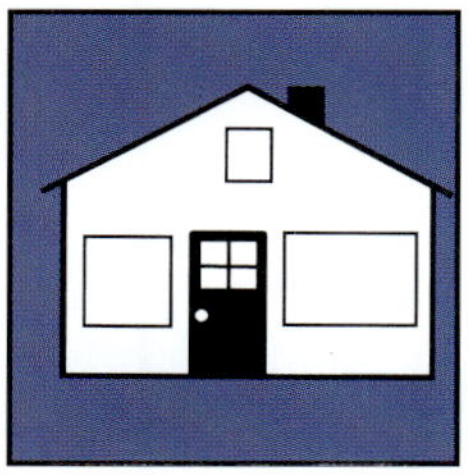

You have learned about homes that people live in. You also learned that people build their homes in many ways because of the different seasons. Are any of the homes you have read about like your own home?

You have learned about the kinds of foods that are eaten in three different countries. Many of the foods are the same as the foods you eat. What else can you tell about the kinds of foods and the way they are eaten in each of the countries studied?

You have learned that families around the world like to have fun. What is your favorite way of having fun?

You have learned about the clothes that people wear in different countries. In each of the countries you studied, there were different seasons. What clothing was best for each season?

Glossary

Australia
Australia is both a country and a continent. It is in the southern part of the world.

bamboo
Bamboo is a stiff, hollow grass.

barbecue
A *barbecue* is an outdoor meal prepared over a fire.

bon appétit
Bon appétit is what French people say to one another before eating a meal. It means, "enjoy your meal."

boules
Boules is a popular game played with large balls and a small ball which serves as the target. The object of the game is to throw the large balls as close as possible to the small one.

canals
Canals are waterways for boats. They are dug across land. Canals let ships travel from one body of water to another.

Canton
Canton is a city in China.

charcuterie
A *charcuterie* is a pork butcher shop.

château
A *château* is a French castle.

chopsticks
Chopsticks are sticks about 25 cm long. Two chopsticks are used to eat food in place of a knife and fork.

continent
A *continent* is a huge piece of land with oceans or seas on all sides.

cotton
Cotton is a cloth made from threads that come from the cotton plant.

cricket
Cricket is an outdoor game like baseball that two teams play with a ball and bats.

Eurasia
Eurasia is the continent that includes Europe and Asia.

grain
Grain is the seeds of plants like wheat, oats, and corn.

houseboats
Houseboats are boats with flat bottoms on which houses are built.

kangaroos
Kangaroos are animals with short front legs and bigger, strong back legs used for leaping.

koalas
Koalas are tailless animals that live in the trees in Australia.

loads
Loads are things that are carried on trucks, ships, and airplanes from one place to another.

lobsters
Lobsters are sea creatures that have two big claws and eight legs. Many people like to eat lobster meat.

Mandarin
Mandarin is the main Chinese language spoken in China.

marché
The *marché* is an open air market where vegetables may be bought.

menu
A *menu* is a list of food served at a restaurant.

ni hao
Ni hao is the Mandarin Chinese way to say hello.

Panda
The *Panda* is a bearlike animal that is white with black legs, shoulders, and ears.

Perth
Perth is a city in Western Australia.

rugby
Rugby is a game like football. The rules let the players carry the ball in their hands.

sheared
A sheep has been *sheared* when all its wool has been cut off.

soccer
Soccer is a game played with two teams on a field. Players try to kick a round ball into a goal.

station
A *station* is a large farm or ranch in Australia.

sty
A *sty* is a place where pigs are kept.

tennis
Tennis is a game played by two or four players. Most often it is played outside. Players use a paddle made of strings to hit the ball over a net.

uniform
A *uniform* is a special outfit that shows that the wearer belongs to a group.

verandahs
Verandahs are outdoor decks. They are covered by the roof of a house.

wombat
A *wombat* is a small Australian animal that carries its young in a pouch.

woven
Cloth that is *woven* has been made by weaving or twisting threads into fabric.

The Young Pioneers
The Young Pioneers is a club that many children in China belong to.